T0197417

Empowered To Lead
Determined to Succeed

LEVEL ONE
WORKBOOK

Empowered To Lead

Workbook

LEVEL ONE
GOAL SETTING

INFINITE POSSIBILITIES INC

www.infinitepossibilitiesvi.com

Copyright © 2016 Michelle D. Mardenborough.

All rights reserved. No part of this book may be used or reproduced by any means,
graphic, electronic, or mechanical, including photocopying, recording, taping or by
any information storage retrieval system without the written permission of the author
except in the case of brief quotations embodied in critical articles and reviews.

Scripture taken from the King James Version of the Bible.
Artist Name - IMAjYNdesign

Photographer Name – Chic Photo

Artist Name for Cover Layout - IMAjYNdesign

WestBow Press books may be ordered through booksellers or by contacting:

WestBow Press
A Division of Thomas Nelson & Zondervan
1663 Liberty Drive
Bloomington, IN 47403
www.westbowpress.com
1 (866) 928-1240

Because of the dynamic nature of the Internet, any web addresses or links contained in
this book may have changed since publication and may no longer be valid. The views
expressed in this work are solely those of the author and do not necessarily reflect the views
of the publisher, and the publisher hereby disclaims any responsibility for them.

Any people depicted in stock imagery provided by Thinkstock are models,
and such images are being used for illustrative purposes only.
Certain stock imagery © Thinkstock.

ISBN: 978-1-5127-1307-7 (sc)
ISBN: 978-1-5127-1306-0 (e)

Library of Congress Control Number: 2015915600

Print information available on the last page.

WestBow Press rev. date: 12/1/2016

Dedication

*F*irst and foremost I thank God for the mission He has given me.

- ◎ To glorify God in my existence.
- ◎ To live a life that reaches its fullest potential.
- ◎ To be a good steward over all that God has blessed me with.
- ◎ To continually seek wisdom and understanding through the Word of God.
- ◎ To walk humbly in love towards others and encourage my circle of influence to do the same.
- ◎ To advance the Kingdom of God through evangelism and soul winning.
- ◎ **To be the best me I can possibly be!**

I dedicate this book to my daughter Satyn-Nishon Geary and every individual who is determined to fulfill their God given purpose in life no matter what challenges and obstacles come their way they remain steadfast, committed, and unmovable knowing that the possibilities are infinite with God!

Acknowledgements

Early development begins in the home. As children we imitate our parents and often learn lifelong key behaviors from our mother and father. I am especially grateful to my mom, Carolyn Chestnut-Smith and my dad, George Leonard Geary for instilling in me foundational principles based on God. I am forever appreciative of my mom's discipline, insight and guidance and my dad's consistency and stewardship.

I am also grateful for the love, support and devotion of my husband, James Mardenborough, the encouragement and love of my daughter Satyn-Nishon throughout the entire process my grandaughter and sugar baby, Destiny Geary-Lee my covenant sisters and constant circle of encouragement, Minister Ethlyn O. Farrell and Intercessor Michelle Roberts and all the strong, supportive women in my life including my dearest friends Tina Blair and Linda Thompson.

A Note to You,

God has invested so much in you. God created you on purpose to fulfill His purpose on the earth. He has given you a task and assignment that was uniquely designed just for you. No one else can successfully complete your assignment. You are responsible to champion and lead the assignment from start to finish that God has given you. Are you willing to step out in faith and complete your mission?

Beloved, I want to encourage you to answer with a resounding YES! God has called you to this assignment because He knows that you can do it. God wired and fashioned you for your assignment. He has already placed the perfect gifts and talents in you to get the job done. God provided you with a circle of influence and surrounded you with the exact amount of resources required. God has empowered you to lead and by your faith you must be determined to succeed. No matter what obstacles, pit falls or distractions come your way you must have a spirit of a finisher, a never quit mentality. It's never about how you start but always about how you finish.

This series of work books is intended to provide you with the basic foundation of leadership as well as to encourage you to stay the course. Level One focuses on the significance of developing goals. A successful start to completing your assignment is the process of outlining your goals. Goal development is nothing new; just a time tested process that works when you are committed to work the process. I believe it's your time! I know you're ready and determined to fulfill your God given purpose in life and no matter what challenges or obstacles come your way. You will remain steadfast, committed, and unmovable knowing that the possibilities are infinite with God!

Remember with God all things are possible! Mark 10:27

Table of Contents

Introduction xiii

Principle One – Believe You Can 3

Principle Two – Write It Down..9

Principle Three – Goal Management..15

Principle Four – Staying on Course 21

Principle Five – Master the Art of Patience 24

Principle Six – The Motivating Factor 29

Principle Seven – Celebrate Each Milestone..33

Conclusion 35

Introduction

Are you determined to succeed in life; have you given any real thought to what it takes to succeed? Have you taken any steps to move toward success? These questions should motivate you to examine your present situation and think about your possible future. But before doing that, you must define exactly what success means for you. Defining personal success will allow you to set self empowering goals. Your success story will not be the same as someone else's success story however; the process to get there will fundamentally be the same. I believe that success is the progressive realization of a goal or dream. So if you are determined to succeed in life you must begin by establishing goals.

Have you honestly given time to developing your future goals? Do you even know where you want to be in the next five, ten or twenty years? If you answered no, you are not alone. Matter of fact, you are one of many who fail to develop a plan or set goals for the future. Going through life without any goals is like getting into a car and driving without a destination. However, the truth is only 3 percent of Americans set and write down their future goals. The Bible instructs us to ***"Write the vision, and make it plain upon tables, that he may run that read it" Habakkuk 2:2* It is absolutely imperative that you write down your goals.** Recent studies show that the major reasons people fail to set goals are due to the following:

- **Failure to Accept Responsibility**
- **Fear of Criticism**
- **Fear of Failure**
- **Fear of Success**

Notice that the common thread for why individuals don't set goals is fear and failure to act. However, if you are truly determined to succeed in life you must do the following:

- **Push Past Fear**
- **Become a Risk Taker**
- **Take Responsibility for Creating a Plan of Action to Achieve Personal and Professional Success**

Without a plan, your future is unpredictable and lacks positive direction. A written plan can be compared to a contractor's blueprint for building a house. Without blueprints there is no shape or form for the house, no knowledge of what's needed to build the house and no timing or schedule to keep you on track with construction. We too, need a blue print or a plan of action to help us accomplish our dreams in life and the first place to start is to write down specific goals.

If you are ready to push past fear, become a risk taker and take responsibility in creating a plan of action; start today by following these **7 principles** to set and reach your professional goals.

Although, this course focuses on professional development; this process may also be used in obtaining your personal goals.

PRINCIPLE ONE
Believe In Yourself

Principle One – Believe You Can

The very first step to achieving a goal is to believe that you can do it. You will not pass go if you don't believe that you can. It doesn't matter how many people believe in you and realize you have the talent and skills to accomplish your goals, if you don't believe in yourself; you will never reach your goals. Scripture emphasizes that "***if you believe all things are possible" Mark 9:23*** You must believe that you can do or be whatever you set your mind to do. You need self confidence and a realization that it begins with your belief system. However, if you lack the belief needed to achieve your goals, you can build confidence and start to believe in yourself through the following steps:

▲ Positive Thinking

Always think positive, psychologist have proven that negative thoughts destroy character, morale, vision, creativity and a person's passion for life. On the other hand, positive thinkers build character, creativity and a motivation to excel in life. Positive thinking is a choice. You can choose to look at life from a positive, neutral or negative perspective. Start today by choosing to see everything in a positive light. The degree of your success will be in direct proportion to the strength of your positive thoughts. **Read Philippians 4:8**

▲ Positive Association

It's also imperative that you take full control of your association. When I was in school my mother instilled in us that bad association spoils good habits. Very simply put, do not associate with negative people; your association must be positive, forward thinking people. Always limit your association to people who want the best that life has to offer, people who are going forward and who want to succeed in life. **Read 1 Corinthians 15:33**

Positive Conversation

Words are powerful. Your conversation should always be positive, uplifting, inspiring and truthful. You've heard the saying, "if you don't have anything good to say, say nothing at all". That is a very valuable lesson that we all should adhere to. The book of Proverbs state *"All the words of my mouth are in righteousness; there is nothing perverse in them" (Proverbs 8:8)* Positive conversation is a key factor to a positive lifestyle. If your conversation is negative your thoughts will also be negative. So remember to speak well of others, encourage, motivate and inspire others by engaging in positive dialogue and conversation.

Positive Visualization

It has been said that the pictures you create in your mind turn into the reality you possess in your hands. Visualization is powerful. Visualization helps you to see where you are going before you get there; many basketball players use this powerful technique at the free throw line. The player stands at the line and visualizes a successful shot prior to taking the shot. In football, the kicker will visualize the ball successfully going through the goal post prior to kicking a field goal. Both of these practices are visualization exercises. The athlete visualizes the successful shot and kick before it occurs. In setting a goal and believing that you can do it, it's important to successfully see yourself achieving the goal. Another exercise if applicable is to keep a photo of what you want or where you want to be with you at all times; the photo serves as a visual reminder of your goal. For example, in 1994 I personally set a goal to move to St Thomas, USVI. I placed a beautiful picture of St Thomas on my desk and looked at it daily. Each time I looked at the picture it reinforced my desire to move to St. Thomas. Needless to say, I reached my goal and relocated to St. Thomas, USVI a few years later.

Positive Affirmations

An effective means of building self confidence and believing in oneself is to affirm your potential power and greatness daily. Daily affirmations do just that, they solidify your belief in the unlimited potential in you. The average person looks in the mirror and only sees a reflection of their current state; a positive thinker looks in the mirror and envisions who he or she can become. Whenever you affirm yourself, you are increasing your belief system about yourself. We've all heard the saying "the more you hear it the more you believe it" That is a very true statement along with the more you do it the easier it becomes; so with that in mind,start today by repeating the following affirmation about believing in yourself and incorporating a positive lifestyle.

Remember….. You will have what you say

Exercise 1 – Write a personal affirmation on Believing in Yourself.

◣ Example- Positive Thinking

I am a positive thinker. I surround myself with positive and productive people. I choose to be a positive influence with my friends and family. I select my association wisely and refuse to spend my energy on negative thoughts and negative people. I speak words of integrity and truth; my conversation is always uplifting and positive. I will have what I say therefore; I say…

- ☐ **I am a child of God**
- ☐ **I am prosperous**
- ☐ **I am generous**
- ☐ **I am wise**
- ☐ **I am successful**
- ☐ **I am a winner**

Write a Personal Affirmation
(Theme)

Believe You Can!

_____

_____

_____

_____

_____

_____

_____

_____

_____

_____

_____

_____

_____

_____

INFINITE
POSSIBILITIES INC.

Review Principle One

1. What is the first step to achieving your goals?

2. What are the major reasons people fail to set goals?

3. If you're determined to succeed in life what must you do?

4. List five key factors to building self confidence.

5. What can a written plan be compared to?

6. Why is visualization important?

7. What is an affirmation?

PRINCIPLE TWO
Write It Down

Principle Two – Write It Down
A real goal is a written goal. When you write a goal you enter into a contract with yourself. By writing your goals down you create a clear step by step path of success for the future. Better yet, when you have well written, well planned, specific goals, you create an even better chance of reaching your goals. As you write your goals make certain you include as much detail as possible. Vague, unclear goals will lead to failure and frustration, while specific objectives are more likely to lead to success. Principle two will teach you how to write present tense, positive, specific, measurable and timely goals.

◣ First and Foremost Write your Goals in the Present

Write each goal as if it is already completed. For example, "I am a home owner" *not I will become a home owner.* By writing your goal in the present you are training your mind to accept, believe and adapt to the written goal. Another example is "I earn $100,000 annually", *not I will earn $100,000 annually.* The significance is on the present. Put the demand on your faith and belief now!

◣ Always Write Positive Goals

Positive goals are stated in this manner "I associate with forward thinking people," *not I will stop associating with negative people.* Never write your goals in a negative tense. Each time the mind processes a statement it attaches a visual; make certain that the visual is positive by not recalling negative thoughts.

◣ Write SMART Goals

Writing clear, relevant, specific goals is a major factor to your overall success. Your goal should always have its expected outcome stated as simply, concisely and explicitly as possible. Specific goals answer questions such as; how much, for whom, for what? A **SMART** goal is Specific-Measurable-Attainable-Relevant-Time bound. For example, a Vague Goal reads: *I will become an electrical engineer some day.* <u>Specific Goal: I will have a job as an electrical engineer by January 1st making 100,00 per year.</u>

◣ Write Measurable Goals

By setting sharp, clearly defined goals, you can measure and take pride in the achievement of those goals. You can see forward progress in what might previously have seemed a long pointless grind.

Your goal must be measurable in order for you to evaluate your progress objectively and determine when you have achieved the goal. In other words, a measurable goal will measure and gauge your overall success rating. For example, <u>I will read six Business Strategy books by December 30th</u>. This is a specific, measurable goal.

◣ Write Time bound Goals

To avoid procrastination and complacency, your goal must have a precise time frame. Establish reasonable timelines to complete your goal. Make certain you give yourself a realistic time frame with a well thought out deadline. If you are attempting to loose a large amount of weight, give yourself a practical timeframe that includes weekly, monthly and quarterly intervals. These mini deadlines will successfully lead you towards your ultimate goal.

For example:

- ☐ **Long Term Goal I will lose 30 lbs. no later than August 30th by eating a raw diet and exercising 3 times a week for 30 minutes**
- ☐ **Bi-Weekly Goal – I will lose 1 lb. bi-weekly**
- ☐ **Quarterly Goal I will loose 6lbs quarterly**

The above goal is Specific, Measurable, Attainable, Relevant and Time bound.

SMART GOAL

Specific □ Measurable □ Attainable □ Relevant □ Time bound

<u>GOALS</u>

1.

2.

3.

**Remember the goals you set will become your blueprint
and action plan towards success**

Review Principle Two

1. A real goal is a _____ goal.

2. Vague goals lead to _____ and _____.

3. What's the significance of writing goals in the present tense?

4. Why write specific goals?

5. What's the significance of writing measurable goals?

6. What is a time bound goal?

7. S.M.A.R.T is an acronym for what?

PRINCIPLE THREE
Goal Management

Principle Three – Goal Management

Once you've written specific, measurable, attainable, relevant, time bound goals, it's time to put them into action by incorporating your goals into your daily life. Goal oriented people are disciplined people. Goal oriented people are driven by their desires and determined to accomplish them. However, to reach your target you must be willing to focus on the bull's eye. The bull's eye in this case, is your goal. In summary, make certain you manage all the things that interfere with your progress toward your goal. In order to do that, each day it's important to do the following:

◣ Review Your Goals

Reviewing your goals daily is a crucial part of your success and must become part of your routine. Take time to review and meditate on your goals in the morning and before going to bed. Create a daily list of things to do to work towards your goal. Ask yourself questions such as; Have I made positive steps towards my goal today? What can I do to move closer to my goal today? Evaluate your daily activities to make certain they align with your goals.

◣ Reinforce Your Goal

Each time you verbalize your goal you reinforce it in your subconscious. Words are powerful. Your Invisible words create tangible outcomes. A critical step to achieving your goal is to talk about it. Bringing life or death to any situation or circumstance is in the power of the tongue. For example, I would share with my family and friends my goal to relocate to the Caribbean. Each time we discussed it I felt energized and more determined to reach my goal. However, a word to the wise, make certain you share your goals with positive people, people who sincerely have your best interest at heart!

Exercise 3 – Each morning when you wake up read your list of goals and reinforce them by verbalizing them.

If you follow this process everyday you will be on your way to achieving unlimited success in every aspect of your life.

Review Principle Three

1. How do you start putting your goals into action?

2. What are goal oriented people driven by _____ and _____.

3. What questions should you ask yourself daily?

4. Words are_____!

5. Invisible words create_____ outcomes.

6. List a critical step to achieving your goal.

7. What type of people should you share your goals with?

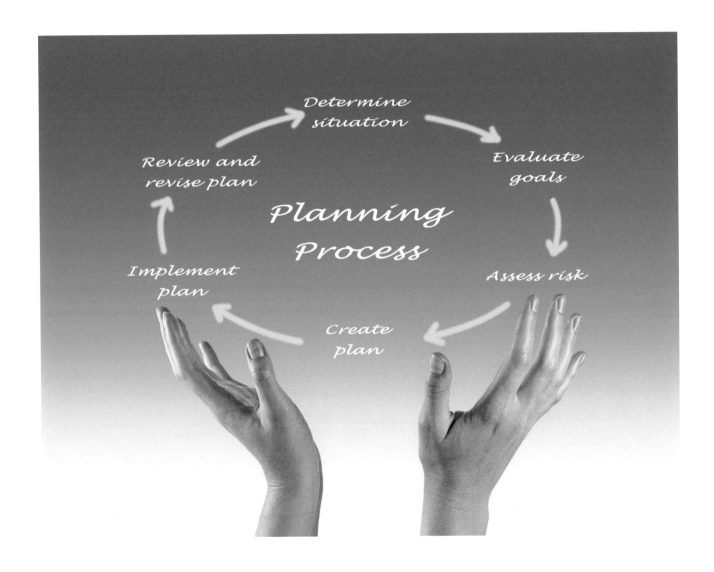

PRINCIPLE FOUR
Staying On Course

Principle Four – Staying on Course

◣ **Don't Quit**

There may be times when you feel like giving up. Don't quit, you have to stay on course toward your goal. Always remember that a major part of staying on course is thinking positive thoughts. A positive, focused and clear mind will keep you on the right track. Keeping a positive perspective on life is very important to your overall success as well as your daily association. Make certain that your inner circle serves as motivation and encouragement for you. So if you face challenges or get discouraged, your inner circle will inspire you to keep going and stay on course and never quit!

Exercise 4 – Write your 2nd Affirmation

INFINITE
POSSIBILITIES INC.

Write a Personal Affirmation
(Theme)

Never Quit

_____

_____

_____

_____

_____

_____

_____

_____

_____

_____

_____

_____

_____

_____

_____

Review Principle Four

1. **What is the major part of staying on course?**

2. **A _____ and _____ will keep you on the right track.**

3. **Make certain your inner circle serves as _____ and _____ for you.**

Special Assignment
by Michelle D. Mardenborough

God has a special assignment selected just for you. God chose you before the foundation of the world to accomplish what only you can do. Your character, gifts and talents are second to none. You have exactly what it takes to get the assignment done. God has deposited and invested so much in you. He sacrificed his only Son to help see you through. So when you get weary as many of us do; stay the course, be a finisher and remain true. You have a special assignment handpicked by God above and no matter the test, you're blessed by the best and covered by the Father's love.

PRINCIPLE FIVE
Master the Art of Patience

Principle Five – Master the Art of Patience

◣ Patience is a Virtue

In today's world patience is a rare commodity. We want what we want and we want it now! People are so accustomed to quick fixes and instant responses that they aren't willing to set goals and work to accomplish them; they're looking for overnight success. However, if you want to be successful and achieve your goals you have to practice a certain amount of patience. True patience requires a willingness to let life unfold at it's own pace. Of course that doesn't mean you sit around and just wait; it means that you put your faith in action and work your plan until you see the manifestation of all your efforts. Creation has a process that cannot be rushed. Consider the farmer; He knows that everything happens in its due season. First and foremost he prepares the foundation; **prior to planting the seed he toils the ground.** Next he plants the seed and waits for the early rains. They are essential because they help the seed to germinate. The seed matures and grows, and in the latter part of the season, the late rains come. The farmer has no control over these things. He must resort to patience. We too, are creating great milestones in our life and we must resort to patience while believing that each goal will be achieved.

Ecclesiastes 3:1-8

For everything there is a season,

And a time for every matter under heaven: A time to be born, and a time to die;

A time to plant, and a time to pluck up what is planted;

A time to kill, and a time to heal;

A time to break down, and a time to build up;

A time to weep, and a time to laugh;

A time to mourn, and a time to dance;

A time to throw away stones, and a time to gather stones together;

A time to embrace, And a time to refrain from embracing;

A time to seek, and a time to lose;

A time to keep, and a time to throw away;

A time to tear, and a time to sew;

A time to keep silence, and a time to speak;

A time to love, and a time to hate,

A time for war, and a time for peace.

Review Principle Five

1. **Patience is a rare _____.**

2. **True patience requires _____.**

3. **Creation has a process that cannot be _____.**

4. **Farmer's know that everything happens in its_____.**

5. **First and foremost the farmer_____.**

6. **We are creating _____in our lives.**

PRINCIPLE SIX
The Motivating Factor

Principle Six – The Motivating Factor

◣ Keep Going and Going

If you are determined to succeed you have to be like the energizer bunny...*keep going and going and going* stay excited, full of energy and committed to accomplish what you set out to do. Don't lose your passion; never allow anything or anyone to steal your joy. If you lose the excitement of achieving your goal, You'll lose motivation to succeed. **Nothing is more important than self motivation and knowing that with "God all things are possible!"**

As you have learned from Principle I, confidence and the belief that you can accomplish your goal is the starting point for success. Putting that belief to action compels you to write the goal down. After writing the goal you have to take responsibility of managing your lifestyle to catapult your written goal into reality. A never quit attitude will keep you focused despite potential distractions; it will also prevent procrastination which is a major decoy. You have to be tenacious, driven, committed and determined to succeed. Don't allow anything to hold you back. You are the motivating factor. You will determine the level of success you obtain; you have to take onus of your life.

The question is; will you? Will you keep going when things get rough, will you stay motivated and determined to achieve your goals, and will you stay positive and productive no matter what circumstances you encounter? I believe you can and I believe you will!

Exercise- 6- Write your personal Action Plan

▶ *Make a master list of the goals in your life; prioritize and date each goal*
Principle-2

▶ *Make a list of steps needed to achieve each goal*
Principle 3

▶ *Make a list of behavioral changes needed to achieve your goal*
Principle 1

▶ *Make a list of new habits that you will adopt to achieve each goal*
Principle 1-7

▶ *Create three Affirmations that you will recite daily*
Principle 1

▶ *Create several reward packages for accomplishing your goals*
Principle 7

Review Principle Six

1. If you are determined to succeed you have to be like the_____.

2. Never allow anyone to steal your _____.

3. Nothing is more important than_____.

4. What have you learned from Principle One?

5. What will a never quit attitude prevent?

6. Who is the motivating factor?

7. You have to be_____, _____, _____, and_____ to succeed.

PRINCIPLE SEVEN
Celebrate Each Milestone

Principle Seven – Celebrate Each Milestone

◣ Celebrate Accomplishments and Milestones Along the Way

There is absolutely nothing wrong with celebrating each milestone that you achieve on the way to accomplishing your overall objective. A celebration serves as a great checkpoint for where you are in the overall scheme of things and motivates you to keep going. It's helpful to plan your celebrations according to the level of accomplishment. For example, if your long term goal is to purchase a car and you have two milestones to reach before achieving your ultimate goal; the first milestone celebration could be dinner at your favorite restaurant, while the second milestone celebration might be a new outfit. Celebrating your accomplishments should never "*break the bank*" but it definitely should give you a great sense of accomplishment. It's also an opportunity to evaluate where you are and to once again start believing for bigger and better dreams. As you accomplish each milestone and each goal you'll realize that all things are possible if you believe. You will actually begin to understand that it's more than just achieving your goals, it's about adopting a mindset and a lifestyle that conveys "the best is yet to come", simply knowing that if you work smart and remain determined to succeed you can accomplish anything!

Exercise-7- For each milestone or short term goal create a victory celebration

Review Principle Seven

1. What does a celebration serve as?

2. It's helpful to plan your celebrations according to the level of _____.

3. Nothing is more important than_____.

4. What have you learned from Principle One?

5. What will a never quit attitude prevent?

6. Who is the motivating factor?

Conclusion

Congratulations!

You have learned seven principles that will help you turn your dreams into goals and your goals into your action plan for success. You have equipped yourself with the knowledge to succeed; we all know that knowledge is power but it only becomes power when we use it. Knowledge without action is dormant power. Have you ever met anyone who is extremely intelligent and full of valuable information but not excelling in life? That's a perfect example of dormant knowledge. The knowledge is available but not being accessed. Don't allow your knowledge to lay dormant; start to put each principle into action right now!

I dare you to put your new knowledge about setting goals into action. Make a definite decision to achieve every goal you set. Be determined; don't allow any distraction, decoy or setback to prevent you from achieving your goal. You are a champion; you have what it takes to win! Go for it, **be determined to lead and destined to succeed.**

All things are Possible with God Matthew 19:26

Every good, productive and positive desire was placed in you by God. He is your Heavenly Father and has your best interest at heart. He wants you to succeed at life. He has endowed you with everything you need to win this race. Whatever vision, dream or goal you have, start with knowing that God is with you and if He is with you all things are possible. No matter how big or small the goal He will see you through. Invite him into your daily processes. Ask Him to order your steps and show you the areas in your life that need to be refined. Listen for His voice of encouragement when you are ready to quit and throw in the towel. Meditate on His Word to strengthen and see you through. Look to His wisdom and counsel to provide insight and guidance. Never let go of His hand. Never give up! Never quit! Stay focused and remember All things are possible with God!

About the Author

Michelle Mardenborough is the founder and president of Infinite Possibilities Inc. a faith based 501c3 dedicated to empowering women to recognize their potential, purpose and destiny through the Word of God and the power of their faith. She is the former host of Women to Women, a local Virgin Islands talk show which empowers and motivates women. In 2010 Michelle launched "**EMPOWERED** for the uncompromising Christian" an electronic newsletter that shares encouraging stories to catapult believers to the next level in Christ. For more information on how you can attend the next Infinite Possibilities Women's Caribbean Beach Retreat or Workshop contact Michelle at www.infinitepossibilitiesvi.com Michelle's rallying cry is "With God all things are Possible."

Copyright © 2008 by Michelle Mardenborough
Empowered to Lead determined to Succeed First edition 2008
All rights reserved

Printed in the United States
by Baker & Taylor Publisher Services